AF513109

Acknowledgement

There are a number of people who have been the source of inspiration for this book. My first and foremost teacher was my mother, who, from an early age, sowed seeds of compassion in me. She is a living example of goodness and love. I must have been five or six-years old when she impressed upon me the dangers of anger. She told me the story of a man who jumped into a well out of anger and could not get out, despite raising it ten times more. Those words of hers still keep echoing in my ears and the picture of the man struggling in the well seems to be engraved in my mind, so much so that anger has been one of the first devils to leave me.

During my formative years, I found myself in a peculiar situation, wherein I had to be good to survive. I just could not afford to throw my weight around. I am thankful to all those people who supported and nurtured me during my formative years. Looking back at it now, I feel there was no better way I could have reached this stage, but through this path.

After my studies, before starting my practice as an eye surgeon, I met a man, who had a tremendous influence on my life. Mr Aporesh Acharya of MILT put me on the right track and stressed upon the importance of the right attitude in life. From then on, one thing led to another—books, people and voices, all kept me moving on this particular path, until one day, something within me urged me to pen down my thoughts.

I have been tremendously influenced by the teachings of Sri Sai Baba, Swamy Chinmayananda and many others, whose writings and lives have influenced my way of thinking. Some of the things that they have written and said have impressed me so much that I made it a part of me and I've put them down in these pages hoping that they would become a part of you too.

It is not easy to put up with a man who thinks differently, for which I am grateful to my wife and children, who have all been my experimental fields and have encouraged and supported me all the way. I am also grateful to

The Power of Love

The Power of Love

Dr K. Bhujang Shetty

wisdom tree

wisdom
tree

WISDOM TREE
4779/23, Ansari Road, Darya Ganj, New Delhi-110002
Ph.: 011-23247966/67/68

© 2005, K. Bhujang Shetty

Reprinted 2006, 2007, 2008, 2009, 2010, 2011, 2012, 2013, 2014, 2015, 2016

All rights reserved. No part of this publication may be reproduced or transmitted in any form or by any means — electronic, mechanical including photocopying, recording or by any information storage retrieval system, without permission in writing from the author and the publisher.

ISBN 978-81-8328-020-4

Edited by Manju Gupta
Designed by Kamal P. Jammual
Published by Shobit Arya for Wisdom Tree

Printed in India

the staff of Narayana Nethralaya for their helping hand in bringing out this book. But the most important person in this whole exercise is **you**. But for you in mind, I would never have written these pages. It was a very clear call from you that encouraged me to share these thoughts with you.

Last but not the least, I must confess that these words are not written by me, but only through me, Him.

Dr K. Bhujang Shetty
info@narayananethralaya.com

Introduction

This book has landed in your hands not by chance, but by choice. You may or may not be aware of it, but at some level you have attracted it. Here we will begin a journey that will take us back to our source. It shall remind us of **who we really are!** It shall reveal to us the purpose of our very existence. This is going to be a conversation between you and me. I have poured out my heart to you in these pages in the most unconventional manner and would love to receive your thoughts and reactions to it.

The very fact that we are human beings means that we have passed all the tests and are in the final lap in this process of realisation. We have all pre-qualified to take up this journey. We could be just a blink away from awakening. Have no doubt about your pre-qualification for whoever you may be and whatever situation you are in now, it is possible to succeed as every sinner has a saintly future.

The very fact this book is before you means that you are the chosen one. These thoughts have come from the heart and not from the mind, so please receive it with your heart. **If you want results, this is not a book to be read, but a book to be lived by**. You may not find anything new here, in fact you may feel that you know it all. What this book is trying to do is to remind you of the facts that you already know but may have forgotten or do not give them the importance that they really deserve. **Our main purpose on this earth is to remember who we really are and later help others to remember the same.**

What we will be doing in these pages is to go through a very easy and a foolproof way of changing our world within, so that the world without changes in our favour. It is foolproof for it has been tried and tested and it is working for me and my greatest pleasure would be to see it working for you. It is not the only way, it is not a better way, but it is just another way.

I am reminded of a story where a villager inherited the most powerful car in the world and ignorant of its use, tied two horses to it and carted the car around in the village. He had the power of thousands of horses inside but he was not aware of it and did not know how to use the power given to him. So throughout life he struggled with it. Aren't we all in the same boat? We are just not aware of the awful sum of power inside us and are struggling throughout life by concentrating on the two horses outside instead of the thousands inside. This book shall teach us to unleash that mighty power inside which created you and me and all of this universe. It could be the turning point in our lives.

To have best of both the worlds.
To have your cake and eat it too.
Read on.

Contents

1

Man and God

Remember, our inner intelligence has greater knowledge than all the doctors in the world put together, for doctors can only treat, whereas healing is from within.

The greatest creation and the greatest gift of all is this human body and the immense intelligence that is reposed within it. It is Nature's most wonderful work of art. Our heart beats about 1,00,000 times a day and about 35 million times a year. It pumps six litres of blood through

120,000 kms of blood vessels in a day. In one second, we are producing 1.2 millions of red blood cells to replace an equal number that die.

Our digestive and metabolic systems have the remarkable ability to transform the food we eat into blood, bone and body structure. The air, which we breathe but cannot see, contains oxygen which is exchanged for the excess of carbon dioxide inside and then thrown out without us even knowing about it. Every time we get a cut or a wound, within seconds there is a tremendous amount of activity in and around the wound to seal and heal it.

The defence system inside us is greater than the defence system of any country. It is greater and more foolproof than the security system around the president of the greatest of nations. The wisdom necessary to fertilise an egg and turn it into a fully grown man or woman is beyond our intelligence. At the helm of this pinnacle of perfection is the brain, overseeing all these miraculous activities.

Now let us look at the other side of ourselves. Imagine yourself typing a letter, while simultaneously watching a TV programme and suddenly you receive a phone call. How well can you perform all the three functions? Definitely not with any high level of efficiency and that's only three activities — while our own inner intelligence is performing trillions of perfectly co-ordinated harmonious activities every moment.

All this clearly demonstrates beyond doubt that there are two sides to ourselves. Do we see them? Do we agree with this? Let us call them the body and the spirit or man and God. Once we become aware of them, we come to believe in them and soon we develop faith in them.

Subsequently, we develop a method to use them for our benefit and that is all this book is about. If there is even an element of doubt, then things just will not work for us. As long as we identify ourselves with the body, we are limited by the body and when we identify ourselves with the spirit, we have an unlimited power and intelligence of the spirit. I am sure all of us want the latter but unfortunately most of us tend to identify ourselves with the body.

In the following pages we shall go step by step on how to align ourselves with the inner intelligence and tap from this unlimited source what we need for our benefit. **There is a genie in us, just waiting to fulfil all our dreams.**

2

Body and Spirit

Remember, we have the power within us to create: Our children are a living proof of it.

The body and the spirit can be compared to the bulb and electricity. The bulb by itself can produce no light and neither can electricity by itself give light, but when electricity runs through the bulb, light is produced. The bulb can be seen whereas electricity cannot, but it can be experienced; the same holds true for the body and the spirit. When electricity passes through the bulb, light is produced; when the spirit expresses through the body, the outcome is life. The very same electricity may pass through various types of gadgets to produce different results.

Similarly, the spirit expressing itself through man, animal and plant, gives rise to the many living creatures found in the universe. To put it grossly, wherever we see life, we see the spirit in action or we could say, **life is God and God is life and everything else** because who else but He can perform millions of right actions every moment in each living organism. This body is like a television set. When plugged into the mains, the television comes alive, but when there is no electricity, it remains a mere box. Just like, when the spirit is in the body, there is life and when it leaves it, although all the physical parts are present, the body is useless and we bury it or burn it at the earliest. For the television to function, it must be well tuned to its source, for the better tuned it is, the clearer will be the picture and voice. An ill-tuned television is just a noise-producing box; it is more of a nuisance and an irritant than a source of pleasure.

When we are not well-connected to our cosmic source and not in tune with the infinite, we, like confused children, having lost our way and forgotten our source, keep mindlessly roaming, not knowing our true selves and our real value.

Having lost connection with our Creator, we tend to fight and struggle for a lifetime. If only we were to sit quietly for a while, contemplate and follow our inner voice, it would guide and reconnect us to our cosmic source and then life would become one beautiful and enjoyable journey. **When we identify ourselves with the spirit in us, we identify ourselves with God.**

The spirit in all human beings and in all living things is the same. This way we get connected and related to every soul on this earth. There is no one else here but ***me***. But when we identify ourselves with the body, then we become different from everyone else. Then there are you and me, two different people. This illusion is the beginning of all tragedies. It is the cause of all the wars that have been fought so far. It is this ignorance that is the root cause of all evil.

Imagine a dog put into a small room which has mirrors covering all the four walls, the roof and the floor. On seeing thousands of its own images in the mirror, out of its illusion and ignorance, the dog barks and bites at itself ceaselessly till it ultimately drops dead, fighting with its own images. This is exactly what happens to us when we identify ourselves with the body. We are fighting and hurting our own selves out of ignorance and illusion. The moment we realise the truth, everything automatically falls into place and we find that the thousands of images around us are our own and we smile and embrace them in eternal love. **Where there is deep love, words are virtually unnecessary as most of the communication is through feelings, which is the language of the soul.**

This leads us to the conclusion that

- **when we forgive someone — we forgive ourselves**
- **when we hurt someone — we hurt ourselves**
- **when we love someone — we love ourselves**
- **when we condemn someone — we condemn ourselves**

When we are angry with someone or want to hurt someone or shout at or criticise someone, just ponder what we are actually doing. We are doing all of the above to none else but ourselves. Life is eternal and there is only one of us here. The day we realise this, the day we totally believe in it, the day we have unflinching faith in it, we stop struggling and start living and on that day, our need for everything else ends. We then move through life as if everyone and everything is a reflection of ourselves and we feel one with everyone and that everything belongs to everyone.

Our earth when compared to the universe is smaller than a tennis ball. Our country may be the size of a small coin, our city may be just a spot and we ourselves a particle of sand. Yet, when compared to the universe, a few of us may not be bigger than a single particle of sand on the sea-shore. Imagine this particle of sand trying to jump with anger, or to act with a vengeance or to bloat with pride! Of what use is it anyway? Who cares for this particle which can be simply blown away by the wisp of a wind?

On the other hand, we are as big as we can imagine. We are exactly as big or as small as we think ourselves to be. Imagine just how many millions of atoms are there in a cell and how many trillions of cells are there in us! While standing on a sea-shore as the waves hit our feet, we feel the mighty ocean prostrate before us, as though it recognises the God in us and only we have the capacity to be aware of it.

3

Why We are in the Present State

Remember, we are empowered to multiply. Our growth from two cells to the trillions that we possess now proves it.

We are all very familiar with the saying **'what you sow, so shall you reap'**. How true it is! If I hurt you, then your most probable reaction will be to hurt me back. If I accuse you, you will accuse me. If I love you, you will love me. It is difficult to hate a person, whoever he or she may be, if that person loves us. **If we will see God in others, then others will see**

God in us. All this is at the gross level. The most important point and the one that is not paid attention to is what goes on in our minds — **our thoughts**.

As we think, feel and believe, so are the conditions of our mind, body and circumstances. The all-powerful subconscious mind which is within us is influenced by our thoughts and beliefs. As we sow in our subconscious mind, so shall we reap in our body and environment. If we sow thoughts of peace, happiness and goodwill and accept them fully in our conscious mind, then we shall reap a glorious harvest. Our subconscious mind may be compared to the soil which grows all kinds of seeds, good or bad. **Every thought is a cause and every condition is an effect**. So, for this reason, it is very vital to take charge of our thoughts so as to bring forth only desirable conditions.

When our mind thinks correctly, when the thoughts we deposit in our subconscious mind are constructive, harmonious and peaceful, the magic working power of our subconscious responds and brings about harmonious conditions, agreeable surroundings and the best of everything. When we begin to control our thought processes, we can apply the power of our subconscious to any problem without difficulty. We actually begin to consciously co-operate with the infinite power, or in other words, we are in tune with the infinite.

Our mind is the link between our body and the subconscious. It is through this instrument that we can influence the subconscious to work for or against us. We need not influence or control anybody or anything outside us to keep us happy. All we need to do is to watch our mind very closely and slowly acquire control over it so that it works in our favour.

All religious processes like prayer, contemplation, meditation, etc. are mere ways and means of influencing our inner intelligence through our mind. For the mind to be controlled, we must first quieten it. Even sitting quietly with our eyes shut for 15 minutes, both morning and evening, will quieten the mind. **An idle mind may be the devil's workshop, but a quiet mind is a God's workplace.**

A mind in peace is heaven.
A mind in pieces is hell.

If we were to only look around us, we will notice that a vast majority of us live in the world without, whereas the more enlightened men and women are intensely interested in the world within. We must remember that it is the world within, that is, our thoughts and feelings, that makes our world without. So every person and everything in our world has been created or attracted into our lives by none other than ourselves. **We are**

responsible for everything as we create our own heavens and hells. If we are not happy with what we have created in and around us, then we have the power to change it.

Most of us try to change the conditions and circumstances which is so very difficult and since the outer world is the effect and not the cause, trying to change it will not produce results. This is the reason why most of us struggle as we tend to work at the wrong end. If we are to have better surroundings, we have to get to the cause and the cause is within us, i.e. **our thoughts and beliefs. Change them and the outer world will change automatically.** Our subconscious mind is very sensitive to our thoughts. Our thought is the parent who gives birth to all things. Our life is the way it is because of the choices we made or failed to make. **Nobody outside us is responsible for our situation. Blessed is the man who finds fault with himself and not with others**.

If we are convinced about the working of our subconscious mind and how it is influenced by our thought processes, let us see how we can practically make use of it in our day-to-day life to get the desired results. Just notice what thoughts and words do to people. To be totally convinced that they are the root cause of everything, we shall analyse the lives of some of our close acquaintances whom we have known for years, like a relative, a friend or a colleague. Take a person who is all the time complaining, condemning, is not happy in whatever situation he or she is, and is always looking at the negative side of things in life. We will notice that his whole life is filled with exactly these things. Somehow or the other, he attracts all the misfortunes. He has enough and more of it to keep complaining about and crying all through life.

Observe another person in your knowledge who is the happy-go-lucky sort. This person is always joking, joyous and happy, laughing and making others laugh, talking of only the good things of life and looking at the positive aspects of everything. His or her life keeps moving that way. He finds enough things to be happy about and thus attracts enough circumstances to be just that.

Notice another person whom you envy. He seems to be having everything perfectly made for himself, as though someone has granted him everything a man could wish for— an ideal wife, loving children, plenty of money, lots of free time, fame and power and is popular with everyone. If we notice his attitude, we will see that he is a totally satisfied person, simply accepts what comes his way, never complains or condemns anybody or anything, is never desperate for anything and all good things just seem to follow him. Do you think that because of all the good things that he possesses, he has developed this attitude or is it because of his attitude that he has attracted the good things in life? Certainly it is because of his attitude that he has attracted all the good things.

When we are totally convinced of the above facts after observing living examples, we must change our attitudes to our benefit. But first we must know the way things work; we must believe in them. If we have even an iota of doubt, if we are not sure whether it will work for us or not, if we make half-hearted attempts, if we do not have the patience to wait for the results, then things will just not work out for us.

What we are today is because of the attitudes we held yesterday and what we will be tomorrow is decided by the attitudes we hold today. Yes, we can foresee our future, as we are the creators of it, although we pretend not to know it.

This universe is a big copying machine, reproducing our thoughts and beliefs in physical forms, that will constitute our experience. This is a big magic show and we are pretending that we do not know the tricks, even though we are the magicians. All the time we live in an illusory world. Our lives are a reflection of what we desire and what we believe we will get. **Even God cannot give us what we believe we cannot have, no matter how overpowering our desire is.**

4

Watching Our Thoughts

Remember, you are the most magnificent, outstanding, remarkable being God has ever created.

Emerson, one of the greatest philosophers of our time, has said, ***'A man is what he thinks all day long.'*** A man's life is what his thoughts make of it. It is rather unfortunate that we have so far not really realised the importance of our thoughts. A man's mind is compared to that of a monkey — always restless, always wandering, never idle. To exercise control over our thoughts, we must first learn to just watch and observe them. Try to see what is going on within. Observe how our mind can never stay on one subject for long. The more our mind is disturbed, the more fickle it becomes.

Nevertheless, even being able to be aware of it is the first step in the right direction. Once we practice this, then we can start analysing what is happening in our mind. We will soon observe that most of our thoughts are concentrated on worrying about the past, anxiety about the future, blaming others for our present state or justifying ourselves for what we have done. How strange that our mind is never in the present! **The past is history, the future is a mystery; it is the present that is a gift — no wonder, it is called the present! The present is all there is, so be in it.**

All sorts of thoughts run through our minds — good, bad and ugly. Since we feel certain that nobody else has access to our mind, we take the liberty to think as we want about any person or thing. This is where we are wrong. **Our minds are connected to each other's and our thoughts have a tremendous influence on the minds that we concentrate upon.** If we consistently think badly of a particular person, then these thoughts automatically attract a similar response from that very person and the reverse also is very true. **So it is absolutely important to think only good of all the people at all times**.

This is absolutely necessary if we want others to think and be good to us. Of course, bad thoughts may occur in the mind now and then, but we must actively try to throw them out and not harbour them for long as they will do more harm to us than to the person we are thinking about. **We may not be able to stop crows from flying over our heads, but we can definitely stop them from building their nests up there.**

While thinking or talking about any person, we must imagine that the concerned person is right in front of us and has access to every thought, every word we utter about him. Would we have then thought or said in that manner? If not, then why entertain such thoughts and words?

This book is all about thoughts, thoughts and more thoughts, because it is our thoughts and beliefs that make up our world. **To have total control over our outer world, we need to control our inner world through our thoughts.** If we are to live in a world of joy, a world filled with happiness and harmony, a loving and a caring world, we need to have similar thoughts as well. **If our thoughts are negative, if our mind keeps harping on harm and failure, on hate and vengeance, on greed and jealousy, how is it possible not to have the same around us**?

People around us behave just the way we expect them to behave with us. Our spouse, children, our superiors, our helpers and the whole world respond to our expectations of them. Have you noticed that when we expect our children to be responsible, they live up to it? When we expect them to be irresponsible, they do exactly so.

You might have noticed that all our subordinates behave in the same manner, for the way they behave has nothing to do with them; it has everything to do with us. So, even though we may get to know new people, their behaviour will be similar to the old ones because the common factor is us. Even our boss is actually controlled by us. If we expect him to be rude and demanding, that is what he will be and if we expect and believe him to be loving and caring and working for our benefit, then that is exactly how he will respond to us. **Our experience is the mirror image of our expectations.**

So, actually the whole world is a puppet show and we are the masters in control. Without being aware of this, we go through life crying and fretting, blaming everyone and everything outside for our present situation, although we are directly responsible for it, as we have created it all. **Fill your mind with good thoughts and good things shall follow you; fill the mind with bad thoughts and bad things shall follow you, for today's thoughts are the seeds for tomorrow's outcomes.**

5

Give and Forgive

Remember, we are created by God and God cannot create imperfect things.

We should forgive others not for their sake but out of our goodness, as vindictiveness is doubly harmful to us. We should treat the so-called bad qualities in man as a misguided God.

A well-guided man is God.

An ill-guided God is man.

So, while dealing with another person, always remember that we are dealing with none other than God Himself. We should see not the person, but the amazing inner intelligence working within the person. If another person does not keep up a promise, we should simply allow him to go his way, make his choice and not force him to come our way.

Whenever we get upset, we must emerge out of ourselves and observe: 'Hey, look, you are upset again! That is not being your true self.' We should be able to watch ourselves. We should not let others control our moods. **We are liked not for our goodness, but for our tolerance**. Every time we get upset, we give the others the power to disturb our mind and when disturbed, our mind loses its balance. Why should we allow others to rule our mind? We should become thick-skinned to the outer world and sensitive to the inner. Acquire total control of the inner to change the outer. It is not possible to change another person, for he is only responding to us. **Masters only act; they never react.**

Whatever we give away comes back to us multiplied — good for good, bad for bad. I have a cousin who is very dear to me, for we both grew up together. He is the one who made me realise that we do not need to have the same parents to be brothers. He had a funny habit of just giving away whatever he had, without any rhyme or reason. We all thought that he was crazy and even to this day he does the same thing. Today he is worth a few hundred millions.

What it means is that we don't become poorer by what we give; instead we become wealthier. This is much more so when we give unconditionally, for then we receive unconditionally and multiply a hundredfold. **We all seek happiness by receiving, but true happiness lies not in receiving but in giving.** This is the law of Nature — try it out.

By giving means we need not necessarily give material things. We can easily give non-material things like love, a smile or a wish. When we wish health and prosperity to others, we indirectly wish ourselves the same. **The easiest way to receive anything is to wish it for someone who needs it**. It automatically comes back to us multiplied. So the next time you condemn someone, be aware of what you are doing to yourself.

Giving non-material things is as good, if not better than giving material things, for when we wish someone well mentally, then we are doing so from the bottom of our heart, without any strings attached, whereas, when we give material things, we most of the time expect something in return. **Motive is everything, for our objectives determine our outcomes**. There is no limit to giving non-material things, for we have unlimited quantities of them.

By helping someone materially or non-materially, we should not consider it as doing a favour. They do not need our favour, for they are gods themselves. It is only an opportunity for us to help ourselves. Whether we encash it or not is our wish.

We have to give to receive and receive to give. We should receive all the good things of life with grace and gratitude. If someone kept on giving us, day in and day out, unconditionally, whether we are good or bad, whether we are black or white, whether we are rich or poor, whether we are aware of it or not, whether we appreciate it or not since the day we were born to the day we leave this earth, what would we consider such a thing? Don't you think it needs to be worshipped? Yes, there are a few things in our lives, which are doing just that, but we have never ever given them any thought. We have taken them all for granted; leave alone thanking them, we are not even aware of them. Our lives would just dwindle away in minutes but for them. They are none other than the sun, the air, the water and the earth. They are the greatest gifts to mankind as but for them, there would be no life. They are a part of Nature. They are a part of God. No wonder our forefathers worshipped them. If we are to be in tune with Him, we must as often as possible thank the sun every time we feel its warmth, thank the air every time we take in a breath, thank Mother Earth for all that she so lovingly provides and thank the water for quenching our thirst.

It is difficult to totally empty the mind, as it has to chew on something or the other all the time. It usually runs back to chewing the same old rotten bones, like hurt, anger, ego, jealousy, lust, etc. Exchange these thoughts with thoughts of gratefulness for the sun, for Mother Earth, for the life-sustaining water and air. **Do not allow the mind to wander, but let it wonder on these wonderful gifts of Nature.**

I was once with a person, whom I consider a master and who was all along telling me as to how overjoyed he was to receive water from his bore-well. He even insisted that I taste a glass of it. I've never met a person who has appreciated and derived so much of joy in a glass of water. That is what masters are made of — they find happiness in small things. **Simplicity and humility are the hallmarks of a master.**

6

Wakeup Call

Remember, the power to be conscious of all his greatness is bestowed only on man.

Our life is nothing but a somewhat stretched version of a movie. All the characters in our lives are as unreal as on the screen. In a movie there is a hero, heroine, villain and supporting characters, all of them put together by the director. **You are the director and the actor in this movie of life.**

While watching the movie, though we are fully aware that it is an illusion, we cry, laugh, get angry, or excited and so involved in it that we tend to forget that it is all cooked up by someone. So also in real life, we do the same thing, taking whatever we see outside as real. The day we wake up, we will begin to laugh at ourselves for having got so involved, for having unnecessarily struggled and fought. Since life itself is an illusion, it is better to sit back and enjoy it as it comes. **We should avoid extreme likes and dislikes and love everyone for what they are, for they are merely playing their roles, which you have allotted to them.**

It is not fair to give someone a negative role and later forget about it and get upset over his behaviour, for he is not at fault, as you are the director of the whole movie and you have asked him to do exactly that. You are upset with the behaviour of the villain in a movie. Just imagine how the movie would be if the villain's role was totally removed. Similarly the ups and downs that we face in day-to-day life make living all the more exciting or else life would be entirely insipid. Even so, all the things that the hero owns in the form of a palatial house, car, jewels, etc. are temporary and last only till the movie is completed. He cannot take them all home. Can he? Likewise, all the things that we own, all the titles that we have earned, all the fame and power that we wield, are all temporary. We don't really own them; we are just their trustees, till the end of this movie of life. **We must get rid of this 'possession obsession'.**

Our family members and all our relatives, friends and colleagues have been brought together for this movie and shall disappear later. **We have been gathered together like a group of dried leaves who will separate from one another at each gust of wind.** We sob and cry at the death of the hero in the movie knowing fully well that in reality he is not dead, but he will be up and alive, shooting for another movie elsewhere. **So, also in real life, there is no such thing as death, for life is eternal and this earth is only a station on our journey to another world.**

Once we realise that the whole thing is an illusion as seen in a movie, we can face all situations happening in and around us with ease. Then we shall realise the folly of jealousy, pride, anger, lust, greed, hatred and attachment. Knowing fully well that all are playing their allotted roles, it would become easy to forgive and learn to love them all. Then life can really become one beautiful journey of joy.

Life is like a dream. When we go to sleep, our real world ceases to exist. Whatever we experience in our dream state, howsoever absurd it is, it looks so very real. On waking up, we laugh at our ignorance and behaviour Similarly, when waking up to reality in life, we learn to laugh at all the things we mistook for real. Then only we take happiness and sorrow, victory and defeat, richness and poverty, success and failure, etc. with equanimity. We cease to have strong likes and dislikes. Whatever comes our way, whether it be good or bad, we take it as His blessings. He knows the reasons for it all. **If we can live our lives without expectations, without preferences, without desires, not only we will achieve mastery over all these, we can also see perfection in everyone and everything.**

If we put an ant on a beautiful canvas painting, what will the ant think of it? Seeing dirty little lumps here and there, irregular and rough surfaces, it would think that it is the dirtiest place in the world. If we were now to lift up the ant to a higher plane, then it would see the beauty of the painting and appreciate its wonderful theme. In the same manner, the bumps and pricks that we experience in life, which we tend to curse, are all because of our ignorance. **We know not the total design of the Creator. A real master never expects or desires anything more than what shows up.** Only when we elevate ourselves, do we see the picture of perfection that's tailor-made for us. It is at this point that we can even love our so-called enemies and say, **'Father, forgive them, for they know not what they do'**, even when they crucify us.

Every time we complain,

we complain against Him.

Every time we are unhappy,

we are unhappy with Him.

7

We are Actors all Day Long

Remember, we have the power to travel faster than light, for our minds can be anywhere in the universe in an instant.

From morning to night, all of us play different roles at different times of the day. In the morning, at home, some of us are a loving father and husband. Later we become the commanding boss in our office. In the evening, with friends, we laugh and joke like children. If we were to observe closely, we would find that we change our behaviour and our make-up to suit our different roles.

A maid comes every day to sweep and clean our place. She works sincerely and is totally dedicated. But while doing her work, she is conscious that it is not her real home. In the evening, she returns home where she really belongs. This is the type of awareness we must have while attending to our daily duties. We don't really belong here and at the end of the day we will return to our original self.

Some of us never like to remove the make-up after some of our roles. Some love it so much that they take it for real and never project their real self. **We all along hide behind a mask, till we totally forget who we really are.** At every stage of the day, we should be aware of the role that we are playing and the real us behind it, never forgetting that we are merely playing a role just as the others are playing their roles in life's drama. **After the scene is over, all of us become equal.** I was once witnessing a scene being shot for a movie wherein the hero kicks and beats up the villain. After the scene got over, I was surprised to see the hero walk up to the villain and touch his feet, asking for forgiveness as the person playing the villain was an elderly, respectable man. So, also in real life, we may not physically touch the feet and say 'sorry' to the people we have hurt, but we can mentally say 'sorry' and ask for forgiveness. This is what is to be done every day just before going to bed. **Ask for forgiveness mentally from all the people we might have hurt while playing our role and forgive those who have hurt us while playing their roles**. This way we become fully aware of the real relationship with others and that all are one and equal.

While dealing with someone, we should never forget that we are actually dealing with God Himself as the intelligence that is in us is present in all others too. **Every time we are with someone, imagine that it is the last time we would ever be with that person and see how our behaviour changes.** When we realise that everyone is an extension of our own self, a part of us, then we immediately attract the other. For example, if we suddenly bump into someone who looks like an Indian in a foreign country, we tend to stop to talk to him and when we find out that he is really an Indian, we feel very close to him. When he tells us that he is from the very state and town that we hail from, then both of us develop a close bond. This is exactly what happens when we see the similarity between ourselves and others.

If only we were to recognise and accept that everyone is but an extension of ourselves, then the forces of Nature would begin to work in our favour.

8

Thoughts, Words and Deeds

Remember, the stability of our outer world is directly related to the stability of our inner world.

All of us have a standing in this society by what we do and say. So everyone gives maximum importance to what we do and say. We are trying to impress people with our words and deeds by not being our true selves. When we express and do certain things, we are all the time doing them only for effect. Most of the time we are playing to the gallery as it were.

Being our true selves is about ending all pretensions. As long as we are still worried about what others think of us, we are owned by them. It is only when we require no approval from outside that we can really become our own selves.

We should say and do things not to please others, not to please ourselves, but to please the Self. We are our true selves only in our minds and thoughts where we never think of pleasing others. Since we live under the mistaken notion that our thoughts are exclusively guarded secrets and have no bearing on others, we tend to indulge in crazy acts. **We forget that our thoughts are seeds, which create our tomorrows.** We have also forgotten that our minds are interconnected to the minds of others and our thoughts influence them positively or negatively, depending on what is going on in our minds. When our thoughts about others are positive, they influence others to be good to us, just as much as doing a good deed for them, for in the mind we are genuinely being good and not just for the sake of it. When our thoughts about others are of anger, vengeance and jealousy, then that is exactly what we should expect in return from them. When a whole nation collectively begins to think that way, it leads to war.

When our thoughts are of one kind, words of different type and deeds all the more different, there is total disharmony in the body, mind and spirit. This disharmony is the root cause of all our trials and tribulations. For our lives to be in total harmony, there has to be harmony in our thoughts, words and deeds. **We must say what we think and practise what we preach.**

If we want to change our outer environment in our favour, then we have to change the type of thoughts we regularly entertain, which is easier than struggling to change our outer world with our two little hands. All we need to do is to take control of our thoughts and that will create and control our outer world. **Success in any field means getting what we want with the least bit of effort. Masters are those who accomplish everything by doing nothing.**

It is easier to perform and achieve success on the mental plane. When we work on the physical plane, we are limited by our body but on the mental plane, the scope is unlimited and the whole universe is there to back us. We can acquire any amount of money, fame, power, etc. on this plane. We can have the world at our feet if we have the belief and faith. We can even move mountains as the power to do so is very much present within us.

We spend most of our time and energy on the physical or the outer world and totally ignore the mental or the inner world. If only we were to switch over to the inner world, we could perform miracles. **Once we switch over and spend more time to control our mind, our need to control other people and possess outer objects automatically reduces.**

What we see and observe on the physical plane is an illusion, so we need not give it too much importance. Learn to live on the mental plane where we can see all as equal, where we can love and embrace all as our own selves, where we can do unlimited service and good to all, where we can grant anyone and everyone all their needs. Learn to spend more and more time on this plane, as on this plane we are truly unlimited and powerful. All the knowledge acquired by man if put together cannot manufacture even a blade of grass; but a baby, the most magnificent creation in the universe, can be brought forth by us with so much of ease and pleasure. **When we work as man, we are limited but when we work as God, we become creators.**

9

Straining to Meet Our Daily Needs

Remember, our brain functions more efficiently than the greatest of computers ever made.

We need not strain to meet our daily needs. If the Creator's eyes are on the sparrow, He will surely care for us. All we have do is to surrender to Him and act. **"The Lord is my shepherd and I shall not want."** When any work is done with this attitude, it becomes a worship, and He takes the responsibility for all our actions. **Our job is only to work and not thirst for the fruit.** The more we concentrate on Him, the more He will concentrate on us and our lives will begin to flow like a wonderful dream. These have been repeatedly promised by all the holy men who have walked on this earth.

Over a period of time, man has conquered his outer world but unfortunately he has totally neglected the more important inner world, which is the prime cause for the present state of affairs. We must take care of the great gifts that He has so lovingly bestowed on us. These are our body, mind and soul. How much time do we spare to nourish these wonderful gifts? We have all along neglected them, taken them for granted and in an illusion, we have spent a lifetime running after toys like money, position and power. If only we were to realise the transient nature of all these things that we are so desperate to possess, we would stop chasing them. **Happy is the man who desires anything, prefers few things, but needs nothing.**

Let us look back on our lives. What happened to the cycle that we as children possessed and admired so much? I still remember the day I bought my scooter. I could not sleep the whole night and the first thing I did in the morning was to run to it, polish it with the cleanest cloth available and admire it the whole day long. I was very possessive about it and would not allow anyone to touch it. I am sure you too can remember similar incidents from your childhood. But then, what happened to them as we grew up? Our love and possessiveness for them slowly faded with time and growth. **When we realise that we are made for bigger things, our desire for small possessions just disappears.** So also the day we know who we really are, the day we realise the transientness of worldly objects, our desires will simply vanish and we would be laughing at all those things that we had earlier cried for. **All the things that we cried for yesterday, we laugh at them today and all the things that we are crying for today, we shall laugh at them tomorrow.**

But nevertheless, as loving parents we do try to fulfil all the desires and needs of our children, although we know that these really do not mean much and sooner or later, our children will realise their worth. Similarly, our loving father gets us all the toys we are crying for today, hoping that one day when we will realise our true nature and our relationship with the Creator, then all our desires for these worldly things will vanish and none of them will really matter. Once we reach that stage, we will stop picking on people's pockets for a piece of bread, or slicing throats for a few pieces of paper, stabbing people in the back for a chair or camouflaging our image to project what we are not. I am not saying that having money, fame and power are bad. We can have as much of them as we want. The only point is that we must know their real value, know them for what they are, so that we don't become a wreck when we lose them. With this attitude for worldly things, we can concentrate on the real issues of importance in our lives.

All of us are chasing worldly needs with just one objective and that is happiness. We believe that happiness lies in acquiring worldly objects like wealth, honour, fame, etc. Actually happiness has nothing to do with any of these. **Happiness is just a state of mind, for we all know that**

the richest people are not the happiest. We have seen how people in power, even the head of a country, can be thrown behind bars one day and may even go to the gallows. **Happiness lies not in having everything we want, but in wanting everything we have.**

Power and happiness that depend on external objects are false. These last only as long as the chair lasts, whereas power and happiness from within are permanent and independent of whether we possess money, title or position. Even when they are all gone, happiness still remains.

Happiness can be obtained from reading unwritten books. These are books written by Nature, which have no language barriers and do not entail hunting them out as they are available everywhere. We should learn to observe and appreciate a flower, admiring its beauty and colour.

The rising of the sun, the gliding and singing of birds, the falling of leaves, the blowing of wind, the running of a stream, waving of tree-tops, the smiles of children — all should arouse a feeling of satisfaction and fulfilment in us. Merely being with Nature for even a few minutes on and off every day will nourish the mind and spirit, for it is at that moment we are really close to ourselves. No wonder golf is such an addiction by playing which we become close to Nature; we become one with ourselves. Observe the intelligence within a seed, which has the capacity to produce a thousand forests. **Whenever and wherever you see a bunch of flowers, accept it with grace and gratitude as a bouquet from the Creator.**

If we really want to be happy, we must find happiness as we are in whatever we are doing right now. **If we are not happy as we are, we**

never will be happy tomorrow or any other day. Our happiness should not depend on any external phenomenon or person. Most of the time we let our happiness depend on others. If someone loses, we are pleased and if others get more than us, we become sad. Why should it be that we let others rule our minds? **Happy is the man who can rejoice at the joys of others.**

We actually have millions of reasons to be happy about if we become aware of all the things that are going right within us. Even the act of going to the toilet can be an act of joy, for being a doctor, I have seen patients writhing in pain on not being able to pass stool and urine. How often do we thank our inner intelligence for having toiled to form and expel all the unwanted stuff with so much ease? The air that we breathe in is usually taken for granted and we all know how asthmatics struggle for every single breath of air. We must jump with joy that we possess all the essentials of life like air, water and sunlight. When the mind accepts this with a sense of gratitude, then it will always be in a state of happiness.

We always think that if we had a particular thing we desired, we would be happy. But unfortunately, it is the other way round. **If we 'can be' in a state of happiness, peace, contentment, etc., then we shall receive everything to keep us in that state. Whereas, if we 'remain' in a state of want, worry, hatred, etc., then we shall receive everything to remain in that very state.**

Observe little children as they run and play; see how they smile and sing all day. They do not sit and worry about what happened yesterday or what they will do tomorrow; they live only in the moment. They can fight and forgive instantly. Infants are a bundle of love and joy; they are gods themselves as we all were a few years ago, but as we grew, **we became worldlywise and heavenly foolish; we changed from God to man.** Since we are gifted with awareness to remember who we really are, we can return to our original self and once again **be the God we were once.**

10

Health is Wealth

Remember, disharmony is the real cause for all illness; harmony is the medicine for all wellness.

The World Health Organisation defines health as a state of physical, mental and social well-being; not merely as the absence of disease or infirmity. We need to take a holistic approach towards health. We abuse most that which we receive free and our body is one such outstanding entity. We realise the value of health only after it is lost. Once lost, no amount of our wealth can ever restore our health for if it was so, the wealthiest people would be the healthiest. We need to lead a balanced life but unfortunately, we have raised our standard of living at the cost of our health, leaving ourselves miserable and sick. **There are a few people on top who are healthy and happy not because of their wealth and power, but in spite of it.**

Possessed by our possessions and ambitions, we become anxious and stressed at the cost of our health. In an attempt to find happiness outside, we increase the complexity of our lives to a point of no return. As can be seen all around us, now it is consumerism that dictates the way we live. Running after money and security, our hearts will never unwind. We need to work to live; not live to work. **When we join the rat race, even if we win, we still remain a rat. Maintaining a healthy inner life is as much a necessity for a healthy body as diet and exercise are.**

The mind plays a very important role in our health. Mental stress is the root cause of most diseases. Stress in life is unavoidable and a little of it is necessary for healthy growth, but when it goes beyond a certain tolerance level, the system breaks down, resulting in illness. Holistic health is not an easy way of living. It is a difficult path as when we suffer a pain in the head or in our stomach or in our joints, we tend to swallow a pill rather than to change our eating habits or give up the deep-rooted hate or fear.

Holistic health is a programme for activating the body's own self-renewal process. It may take years to yield results. It is well known that quite a number of modern man's problems, such as obesity, diabetes and high blood pressure, which are all killers in the long run, are caused by a sedentary lifestyle and habits. Even a moderate amount of exercise regularly will go a long way in keeping this body healthy and improve the immune system within. **It has now been statistically proved that physical inactivity kills more people than even smoking.**

Our health depends not only on physical exercise but also on what we eat. It is a balance between input and output. Most of us suffer from the disease of excess. Problems like diabetes and high blood pressure are all considered as rich men's diseases, created by hurry, worry and curry. Never show your love through the stomach, for by doing this you are causing more harm than good. Mothers who stuff their children with high-calorie, high-fat diet are causing tremendous damage to the health of their children and are sowing seeds of all kinds of diseases early in childhood itself.

It is in early childhood that the parameters or the so-called thermostat is set for our hunger level and quality and quantity of food that is necessary to satisfy us. If we feed a child with all sorts of rich and fatty foods, the child while growing up will crave only for such stuff and later on, no amount of reasoning can get him out of it. In our over-enthusiasm, we kill the child with all the wrong foods when we don't really have to.

The most important aspect of a holistic health concept is relaxation. In normal conditions of life, sleep itself provides sufficient relaxation, but under stressful conditions of modern life, the mind remains in a tense state; and sleep is just not sufficient to unwind. As long as tension persists, the problem can only tighten. Counter measures against stress include certain spiritual techniques, such as prayer, meditation, self-surrender, acceptance, non-judgement, etc.

The popular saying 'early to bed and early to rise makes a man healthy, wealthy and wise', makes a lot of sense. For, it is early in the morning that we can be alone and aware, with no phone calls or appointments disturbing our state of mind. Then we can meet our real self and do some introspection and soul searching. As we keep doing this, we will be led and guided on the journey of self-discovery and inner health. We exhaust ourselves by running after illusions. We spend a whole lifetime building castles in the air, get too engrossed in this outer world and entangle ourselves in this web.

We must learn to be in the world without getting pulled down by it; we must keep our balance constantly and maintain inner peace. We must centre ourselves through thick and thin. Balancing entails finding what our real needs are, identifying our many interests, and then re-arranging our priorities to reflect on those needs, **If we can learn to enjoy whatever, wherever, whoever we are, then situations will not really matter and the struggle will end for us, to begin on a journey of inner peace and harmony. Never forget that ours is a three-million-years-old human body, which constantly heals the daily wounds of normal existence, only if we allow it do so.**

11

How Free are We

Remember, there are no coincidences, no accidents; there are only consequences.

There is a law that precisely describes why life is as it is this very moment. This is the law of *karma*. It is the moral law of justice which gives us what we deserve. Our *karmic* worth is equal to the total of all our thoughts, words and actions in which we are engaged in this and in our past lives.

The Power of Love

What we see and know, what we are right now, our health, our wealth, our family, our finances, our beliefs — everything that constitutes what we call our life is the end result of what exactly we deserve. But what we are not aware of is what produced all this; so we do have an answer but we do not know how we got there.

However much we may try to recollect the causes for our present situation, we may not be able to synchronise everything. As we cannot recollect well enough what we have done in this life alone, how can we remember our past lives? We need to focus on what we need to do to make our lives more productive, more meaningful, happier and healthier.

The principle behind all this is simple. If we sow positive seeds, we will reap fruits of happiness and if we sow negative seeds, we will reap fruits of pain. But many of us are unable or unwilling to give up the present ounce of pleasure to gain a future pound of happiness or avoid a like measure of pain.

The law of Nature works whether we know it or not, believe in it or not. Like the law of gravity, it acts without exception, so also does the law of *karma*. The law of the land punishes the guilty only if caught, tried and proved whereas the law of Nature is inescapable. Everything is totally accounted for and perfectly tallied. It is self-executed and unavoidable.

The *karmic* law continuously balances our account of good and bad. We need not know everything about a car's mechanism to be a good driver; similar is the case with the *karmic* law. We only need to learn how to drive our lives. Everything is happening just as it should and if we firmly believe that a higher power, the cause behind all causes, is always fair and impartial and everyone gets what he or she deserves, then we will stop complaining and start correcting ourselves for a better tomorrow.

We should accept that our present situation is a product of our past; no matter what we are and where we are, we alone are responsible for our present. There is no point in crying and fretting that the world is unfair. **It is a marvellously just world; a world that already is and will always be in perfect harmony.** All problems that we experience arise from ourselves and not from outside, yet we keep asking how it is possible for the universe to be perfect and harmonious when there is so much of pain and suffering.

Everybody knows what is right and what is wrong. 'Smoking is injurious to health' is printed on every packet, but what is it that compels the smoker to pick up a cigarette in spite of scientific proof of its danger to health? It is nothing but our past actions that compel us to think and act as we do, and get caught in the crossfire. It's our past actions that have put us in the situation we are in now, like the time and place of our birth, our parents, our environment and everything surrounding us.

If that is so, then what is the way out? Are we totally helpless? Yes, the past is past, we cannot do anything about it, but what we can do is to attend to our tomorrow. If we want a better tomorrow and I am sure all of us do, we need to watch and do the right things the right way today itself. But then, who is to judge what is right and what is wrong, for both are a matter of perception.

If we really dig deep into our actions, we will find that none of them were totally selfless, for at some level we had an axe to grind. It may not be in the form of money; it can be in the form of name, power, recognition, etc., which may have produced *karma* in the form of negative actions, and we are caught in this never-ending vicious cycle. It is also unfortunate that none of us can be totally actionless for we are all compelled to take some action or the other. And if this be the case, then what is the way out? Yes, there is a way out and it is a very, very simple one.

Once a man asked the Lord as to who was his favourite devotee and the Lord gave directions as to where the man could find this devotee. Eager to know who it was and how he had gained the grace of the Lord, the man rushed to the place the Lord had indicated. He searched in that particular place but could find no saint or holy man. So he went back to the Lord to reconfirm the address. The Lord repeated the same place. So the man went back and searched all over again. All he could find was a farmer leading a normal life. Anyway, the man enquired of the farmer as to how often he went to the temple and how often he prayed, etc. The farmer replied that neither did he visit any temple and nor did he pray. The man, surprised, rushed back to the Lord and expressed his doubts on his dearest devotee. The Lord said, "Yes, it is the farmer who is very dear to me." The Lord asked the man to go back and enquire further. This time the man sat with the farmer and asked him how he was so dear to the Lord without even visiting a temple or remembering the Lord. The farmer replied, "You remember a person only when you forget him, but where is the question of remembering the Lord when I never ever forget Him? He is there at every step and in every breath of mine."

This is the story that changed my life forever. I thought that it was not too tall an order to perform. One need not go miles in search of Him. All we need to do is to train our minds to meditate on Him every moment of our lives until we see Him in everyone and in everything. **He has given us the time, space, cause, material, idea, skill, chance and fortune. Why then do we feel as if we are the doer?**

If we are held responsible for every action that we perform, the best way is to transfer the responsibility to someone else who is willing to bear the cross for us. And who else but the Lord is ever willing to accept it, if only we were to ask Him? To do this we need to **surrender and offer every action unto Him before performing it and He will willingly take on the responsibility for the outcome of such an action, as it has been done as an offering unto Him.**

For this we need to have Him on our mind at every step of our life, with every breath that we take, every morsel of food we eat and every act we perform. Perform every action in the form of a prayer and be grateful for having been given the opportunity to serve the Lord through your action. Never let the mind wander from the thought of the Lord at any moment of the day; let everything and anything remind you only of Him and He will take the total responsibility for everything you do. Slowly but surely, our past baggage will reduce and our tomorrows will become better.

We should see the Lord sleeping in the mountains, smiling in the flowers, singing through the birds and up and awake in man. We need to see Him by default like a screen saver. The mind needs to be grounded and rooted on the Lord. All this is possible only if we have unflinching faith in Him.

The following story brings tears to my eyes every time I read it:

One night a man had a dream. He dreamed that he was walking along with the clouds. Across the sky flashed scenes from his life. For each scene he noticed two sets of footprints on the sand: one belonging to him, and the other to the Lord. When the last scene flashed before him, he looked back at the footprints in the sand and he noticed that many times along the path of his life, there was only one set of footprints. He also noticed that this happened at the very lowest and saddest moment of his life. This really bothered him and he questioned the Lord about it, "Lord, you said that once I decided to follow you, you would walk with me all the way. But I have noticed that during the most troublesome times in my life, there is only one set of footprints. I don't understand why, when I needed you most, you would leave me."

The Lord replied, "My son, my precious child, I love you and I will never leave you, during your times of trial and suffering. When you saw only one set of footprints, it was then that I carried you."

When such is the love of the Lord, what should be our response? **Our hearts and minds will always be where our treasure is. If we put all our treasures on the Lord, then the mind will rush back to the Lord every other moment.**

The modern man with all his achievements does not seem to be happier than his ancestors for he is not more virtuous than them. This is a proof that we are protected not by our possessions, but by our virtues. If we want a better tomorrow for ourselves, for our loved ones, it cannot be guaranteed by our planning, by our riches, by our connections, but only by living a righteous life and above all, seeing Him in everything and everyone.

Let's not forget that we have all come to serve a term. One term may be a simple term; the other may be rigorous one for what we have done in our past. The least we can do is to be kind to all, for each one is struggling and fighting a battle of his own. We are all carrying a baggage of our past and in our ignorance of how to lighten it, we add to it and get caught in this vicious cycle.

In Nature there are neither rewards nor punishments; there are only consequences and consequences are precise, unavoidable and unchanging. As a result, we are punished, not for our sins, but by our sins. Whatever we do, whatever we eat, whatever we sacrifice, whatever we give in charity, whatever we perform, we must do it as an offering to the Lord.

12

Everything is His Grace

Remember, we have won a big race by beating millions of sperms to fertilise the lone egg in our mother's womb.

Everything, from this magnificent body to every breath of air that we breathe, is all from the Creator, totally free, unconditionally provided to us by Him. If we could only realise this and appreciate it in our daily life, then every moment of our life would be filled with nothing but gratitude, which is a state of being with Him. Every morsel we eat, every drop we drink, every little help that we receive from a fellow-being, we shall take it as provided by Him. It is only when we feel that we must get a particular thing as our birthright or since we have paid for it, we get upset and feel cheated. If we were to accept them as they really are, then we would be ever grateful for everything and to everyone for He Himself has come to us in the form of our servant, driver, watchman, gardener, neighbour, relative, friend, child or spouse.

We should look upon each person in our vicinity as doing us a favour and be ever grateful for it. We should not see the person but look at the inner intelligence within the other to be aware of the God we are dealing with.

When we are in trouble or depressed, we need not go to any place or person, for help is at hand. It is closer to us than we could ever imagine, for it is within us. **Whenever there is a problem, there is not only something to do, but also to know and learn, for there is a hidden opportunity in each crisis.** Think back a few years when we were just two-cells old, still within our mother's womb. Who or what protected us? We could have been drowned by a drop of water. Who was it that guarded us and made us into this mighty human being? Have faith in that force within that helped us, whether we like it or not, whether we are aware of it or not, whether we accept it or not, for we are the loving child of this almighty force.

Prayer is a communion between us and this mighty force, but it usually turns into a begging session for our endless wants, which is not necessary because He is aware of our deepest desires. The best way to fulfil our wishes is to be and act as though it is already granted to us and thank Him in advance for doing so. In every likelihood it shall come true. **So, a prayer should be a session devoted not to asking for ourselves, but of thanksgiving for all the things we have already received and all the things we hope to receive.**

We should count our blessings and name them one by one, whenever our mind is free. **A grateful heart is always dear to God.** Thank the God that we have two eyes to see, two ears to hear, two legs to walk on and a tongue to talk. Thank the God that we have a memory that can remember alphabets and put them together to read words. If we start to think about all the good things we possess, the list will never end. A lifetime is not sufficient to thank the Lord for all His goodness bestowed upon us.

Whenever we see a physically challenged person, we should immediately thank God that we are normal and pray for the disabled one. We must be grateful that He has made us into human beings, His greatest of creations, and not into anything else. Realise that the millions and millions of co-ordinated activities that are going on inside us are not by accident. It is the handiwork of the Almighty. Acknowledge it, appreciate it and be grateful for it. Don't ever take anything for granted.

Before drinking or eating anything, bless it and give thanks for it. Just imagine all what must have taken place and all those who must have been involved in providing us this drink or food. The earth that grew it, the water and the sun without which it would not have survived, the farmer, the vendor and the cook, all have played their part. But we, in our mighty ego, think that we have paid for it and it is our right not only to have it, but also to waste it. Always accept it as a gift from all concerned and mentally thank them all, for **gratitude is the attitude that makes one humble.**

If ever we need help, there is no point in going out in search of it, for there is no person or place better than the one within us. **Doing so would be like being a fish going in search of water.** Our inner intelligence makes us do the right acts; can't it provide us with our basic needs? The only thing is that we must be tuned or in alignment with it. Once in that position, it is like hopping on to a train. There is no point in carrying our luggage on our head once we have boarded the train. We have to simply unload all our troubles down from our heads and enjoy the journey. While sailing in a small boat, we are tossed and turned in by the smallest of waves, but once inside a big ship, though we may not be able to avoid the waves, they cannot disturb us. So also in life. When we are one with Him, though the waves, like the ups and downs of life are present, they hardly affect us.

The problem is, we seem to know it all. There seems to be nothing new about what we have discussed here. We have either heard or read it somewhere before. **Knowing is not doing; doing is doing.** We have to put them into practice before it can work for us. Once we taste the sweet success of practicing it, we may never look back. **Masters may look like ordinary men from the outside, but they are giants within.** It may take some time, but we must not grow impatient. It is better to let a rose bud blossom into a beautiful flower naturally with time than to force it to open immediately into an artificial one.

A realised soul is a person who has realised that he is God; **so, when we accept and have total faith in Him, who is not out there, but in here, then we become a God. A realised person.** It is as simple as that. The very purpose of our existence is this and once we realise it, we must help others to achieve the same. **Everything else in life is secondary and nothing else really matters.**

A realised soul is one who can see
success in failure and failure in success,
good in the bad and bad in the good,
life in death and death in life,
method in madness and madness in method,
all in one and one in all.

13

When in Tune with the Infinite

Remember, God Himself is waiting within us to be expressed through us.

When we are in tune with the infinite, things start to happen automatically, without any effort on our part. **Life gets into an auto mode.** We get magnetised and people love to be in our company. They begin to share their innermost secrets, their joys and sorrows with us.

We suddenly find that we have all the time in the world to do all the things we ever wanted to do. We seem to have the money that is necessary and all the love we require. We tend to move around with a certain glow; the glow of the divine. We simply love everyone and everything, and in turn everyone loves us. All our needs and deepest desires are spontaneously fulfilled. We feel joy, happiness and vitality in every moment of our existence. Situations and circumstances make our life a bed of roses.

Whenever we encounter a problem, we feel confident that the power within us can easily handle it and that it will be solved with ease. **All the things that we were earlier chasing like money, fame, power, etc. will now start to chase us.** Life starts working the way we always wanted and things just keep falling into their proper place. We seem to be doing the right things at the right time. The gap between our thinking a thought and it being manifest begins to shrink and finally it will disappear totally, producing results instantly. We start receiving help from unknown sources; even our car tyre will puncture only at a place where help is on hand. Do not take even the smallest of these happenings as just an accident or coincidence, as there are no accidents; all of them are the consequences of our thoughts and beliefs. So, only if we could change our attitude, we could change our world.

Every time we re-read a book, we don't find more in the book than we did before, but we find more in ourselves than we had before. At the end of this chapter are ten statements which can change our lives. They are statements which summarise all that we have discussed so far. If we wish to sit in the driver's seat and acquire total control of our life, all we need to do is make them a part of us. We could do this by spending 15 minutes in the morning and evening reading them, contemplating on each one of them for a minute. Choose one of the statements each day and dwell upon it throughout the day. Repeat that particular statement as often as you can in your mind during the day, maybe a few hundred times. This will allow it to sink into your subconscious. Once it sinks in, it becomes a part of you. Do this for every statement and soon you will be guided and led by each of them. **For every step we take towards Him, He will take ten steps towards us**. Soon we will notice that He leads us, helps us, holds us all the time till we become a part of Him and we once again **be the God we are.**

Goodbye and good luck.

God willing,

some day, somewhere,

we shall meet.

- **I am not this body, I am the spirit.**
- **I surrender to Him and act.**
- **I am happy as I am.**
- **I am ever tolerant.**
- **I am ever grateful.**
- **I accept things as they are.**
- **I see God in all and God for all.**
- **I see not the person but the intelligence within him.**
- **I see an opportunity in each crisis.**
- **I live neither in the past nor in the future; I live in the present.**